How To Analyze People

Get The Best Out Of Every Conversation

Kevin Bradnik

Copyright © 2016 Kevin Bradnik

All rights reserved.

ISBN: 1540774929
ISBN-13: 978-1540774927

© Copyright 2016 by Kevin Bradnik - All rights reserved.

This document is geared towards providing exact and reliable information in regards to the topic and issue covered. The publication is sold with the idea that the publisher is not required to render accounting, officially permitted, or otherwise, qualified services. If advice is necessary, legal or professional, a practiced individual in the profession should be ordered.

- From a Declaration of Principles which was accepted and approved equally by a Committee of the American Bar Association and a Committee of Publishers and Associations.

In no way is it legal to reproduce, duplicate, or transmit any part of this document in either electronic means or in printed format. Recording of this publication is strictly prohibited and any storage of this document is not allowed unless with written permission from the publisher. All rights reserved.

The information provided herein is stated to be truthful and consistent, in that any liability, in terms of inattention or otherwise, by any usage or abuse of any policies, processes, or directions contained within is the solitary and utter responsibility of the recipient reader. Under no circumstances will any legal responsibility or blame be held against the publisher for any reparation, damages, or monetary loss due to the information herein, either directly or indirectly.

Respective authors own all copyrights not held by the publisher.

The information herein is offered for informational purposes solely, and is universal as so. The presentation of the information is without contract or any type of guarantee assurance.

The trademarks that are used are without any consent, and the publication of the trademark is without permission or backing by the trademark owner. All trademarks and brands within this book are for clarifying purposes only and are the owned by the owners themselves, not affiliated with this document.

FOREWORD

I want to thank you and congratulate you for downloading the book, *"How to Analyze People: Get the Best out of Every Conversation."*

Anyone who has been around other people already knows that they can seem mysterious. It's possible to spend many hours of our lives puzzling over what someone said or did, trying to figure it out. When you learn how to analyze other people, this struggle disappears. There are several factors at play here, which will be covered in this guide. A couple of these factors include:

Reading People using Words:

This one may seem obvious, but there's more to it than you think. What can be learned not only from the words people choose to use, but the hidden messages behind them? We will explore this question in the following pages.

Interpreting Body Language:

Most of what we say is nonverbal and comes across from the rest of our body, including our facial expressions and tone of voice. Even our feet and arms are reliable indications of how we truly feel!

Understanding yourself:

You may consider self-analysis as a separate subject altogether apart from analyzing others, so you might be surprised to learn that they, in fact, go hand in hand. In order to read others accurately, you must first understand your own psychology and feelings. This book will tell you exactly how to do this.

Contents

Chapter 1: How Analyzing People Helps you   1

    Successful People are already Aware of this Power: 1

    Anyone can Learn this Skill: 2

    What are the Consequences of not Learning this? 2

    How to Approach this Information: 4

    It's about Knowledge, not Judgment: 6

Chapter 2: Using Words to Analyze People   8

    How Using Words helps with Analyzing People: 8

    Looking at the Extra Words People Use: 10

    What do these Extra Words show us? 10

    Examples of Clues in Choice of Words: 12

    Introversion vs. Extroversion: 15

    Using this Knowledge to Read People: 17

Chapter 3: Interpreting Body Language Signals   20

    The Body's Role in Expressing Thoughts and Feelings: ... 21

    A Summary of Body Language Cues: 31

    Body Language Myth vs. Truth: 34

Chapter 4: Using a Comfort vs. Discomfort Spectrum — 41

The Comfort vs. Discomfort Spectrum for Understanding Body Language: 42

Situations for Gauging Comfort Levels: 45

Chapter 5: Understanding yourself First — 49

What do Unrecognized Emotions Result in? 49

How to Learn More about yourself: 51

Becoming Aware: 52

Conclusion — 59

Chapter 1: How Analyzing People Helps you

Although you may find this topic intriguing, you might wonder how this knowledge can be of practical use in your life. To put it simply, a whole new world of possibilities opens up to you when you learn how to read the behavior and feelings of others. Situations that once threw you into a confused state of mind with seemingly no way out will no longer be an issue for you. Dealing with "difficult" people will no longer be a source of stress and misinterpreting the wants and needs of others won't mystify you anymore.

Successful People are already Aware of this Power:

People who enjoy successful love lives, profitable money situations, and careers already know all about the life-changing and critical power of analyzing others confidently. However, this pursuit is not always so easy. For some of us, this is not an intuitive skill, and most people find that they have to study it quite intently to begin getting a grasp on the subject.

Anyone can Learn this Skill:

The great news here is that all people can learn the hacks, tricks, and skills needed for becoming great with reading and analyzing others. The incredible power behind seeing what a person is truly thinking can be gained by any person who discovers the secrets of analyzing others.

What are the Consequences of not Learning this?

- **Job Complications:** When you are unaware of how to read others, you are more likely to run into conflict at work. If you have ever wondered why your boss seems to have it in for you, or why you can't seem to make yourself clear to your co-workers, this information will help you immensely.

- **Personal Relation Problems:** Without knowing how to read your partner, a healthy and happy relationship is impossible. You will likely find that fights last a lot longer than they should, or that you simply don't know how to fix problems when they arise until you learn this valuable skill. Do you get into fights with your spouse and stop halfway through to realize that you don't know what you're fighting about or how to solve the problem? This can be helped by learning how to analyze others.

- **Trouble Understanding yourself:** True analysis of human behavior does not just entail reading others, but also knowing how to read ourselves. To be frank, without understanding yourself, life is going to be a struggle for you. And there is little to no hope of learning how to read other people if you haven't first figured out how to understand and read your own feelings and thoughts. Since this is a key factor in learning to analyze people, we will cover this in depth in the last chapter of the book.

The foundation of unlocking true connections with people, personal success, and real happiness is yours to take as soon as you become aware of some simple factors of body language and basic psychology. You can free yourself from the inherent limits of everyday communication by understanding the world in a deeper way. Don't allow yourself to be held back by your inability to read others.

How to Approach this Information:

Before you can gain benefits to knowing the information you are about to be given in this book, you need to know how to approach it correctly. Here are some considerations to keep in mind:

- **Use Observation plus Experience:** Although skills of observation are valuable and absolutely necessary when it comes to analyzing people, they won't be of much value to you unless you combine it with personal experience. This combination will aid you in learning to tell personalities and types of people apart from one another. It's impossible to take one single formula and apply it to every person or even their every trait.

- **Humans are Complex:** Knowing more than others about analysis of behavior will put you miles ahead of other people, but keep in mind that humans are complex beings. There is not a simple method for knowing everything about everyone, all the time. And any approach to learning more about this takes time and effort. Like any other skill, it takes patience and practice.

- **Interaction helps you Learn more:** Gaining conceptual knowledge through reading about a topic, for example, is helpful in learning about any given subject. But interacting with people is another great way to learn how to interpret them. This can involve eating with the person at a restaurant or simply going out for a walk. During this activity, you can keep a close eye on their mannerisms, how patient they are, as well as their general temperament.

    Being in either a casual or professional situation with someone else will help you understand the way they function in various scenarios, along with how they normally act on a day to day basis. You can supplement this general observation with strategies about whether they prefer to work as a team or on their own, and to test their factual awareness.

- **Try not to Assume:** Although it's nice to learn how to read other people, it's important not to assume too much. Although you may get quite good at interpreting how others feel and the thoughts they think, it's always best to check for confirmation before you assume anything for sure. Look for multiple clues, including context and past behavior, in order to form a solid opinion and then try to test this by asking them for confirmation or observing their behavior to see if you were right.

It's about Knowledge, not Judgment:

Don't mistake the art of getting to know the thoughts and habits of others as a way of judging their character. Along the way, you will learn how to interpret other people, but don't allow other people to judge your willingness to learn or know. This is a good habit to form, one that can help you stay aware of the personality types constantly surrounding us in daily life. All people are ultimately different from one another; but by gaining understanding of them, we widen our perspective and abilities in general.

Chapter 1: How Analyzing People Helps you

Chapter 2: Using Words to Analyze People

Although nonverbal communication (aka body language) is an important way to interpret the meanings behind the words of people, words should never be ignored. The first most obvious and basic way to analyze people is to look to the words they use. What clues are hidden within how they speak? Words are symbols meant to represent the thoughts we have, and the closest it is possible to get to someone else's ideas is to read or listen to the words they choose to use.

How Using Words helps with Analyzing People:

- **Personality Cues:** The words that people choose to use reflect the characteristics of their personality. These can be seen as clues to what lies behind that person's demeanor. After getting to know someone over a period of time, you will likely notice that they have certain habits of speech or favorite words that they like to repeat throughout the day. Although this is better and more easily seen when you know someone on a personal level, to a keen observer, it can also be noticed in mere acquaintances or even strangers.

- **Prediction for Behavior:** When you get familiar with the clues inherent in the words of others, you can better predict how they will behave in the future. Learning to analyze others is all about gaining knowledge that will benefit you, and learning how to predict the behavior of others will help immensely in this regard.

- **Insight into Thoughts:** Although you cannot determine someone's full personality by just listening to their words, you can gain valuable insight into the way they think by knowing what to listen for in their choices of words. You can also discern how they wish to be seen by other people, which gives you insight into the type of person they are and what they value in life.

You can develop ideas and hypotheses about the clues in people's words and apply additional information that you have about that person, either first hand or from other sources.

Together, this can form a holistic picture of their personality or ideas. Our human brains are amazingly efficient and complex, and even seemingly insignificant expressions that people make can show us a lot about who they are on the inside.

Looking at the Extra Words People Use:

Each time a person thinks, he or she can only use nouns and verbs to formulate thoughts. The more complicated additives, such as adverbs and adjectives, are added to these thoughts once they are either written or spoken. It is these added words that can lend insight into a person and how they work, think, and act. Your basic average sentence will have a verb and a subject, describing the person and the action that person is doing. Any words added on top of the simple explanation of who did what can show characteristics and give personality cues of the writer or speaker.

What do these Extra Words show us?

Clues such as these extra words let people observing to form hypotheses or guess about the personality traits of the speaker. In a sentence that describes someone walking, for example, if they add the word "quickly", it would show that they experienced some urgency, without giving a reason.

- **Paying Attention to Context:** You can learn a lot about someone by listening, not only to the specific words they use, but the reasons they give for their actions. Someone may, for example, walk "quickly" due to being late to work, and use a descriptive term such as this to tell you how they walked earlier that day.

- **What do their Words say about Them?** People who want to be seen as conscientious and reliable would walk quickly to make it to their appointment or shift at work. If someone takes the time to walk fast somewhere, they likely care about how others will view them and have respect for the norms that we all live with on a social level.

- **Why did they Choose that Word?** Although there are many different reasons why someone might describe their way of walking as quick, there is a very specific reason behind their choosing that particular word.

Seeking clues behind people's words is a technique that is not invasive and allows you to read people effectively, without them knowing about it. How else can paying attention to word cues give you valuable insights about the people you are attempting to analyze?

Examples of Clues in Choice of Words:

- **"I Won Again":** The choice of the word "again" shows that the person saying this had already won before, at another time, and that they want the people to whom they are speaking to know that they have won before. In other words, they are attempting to improve how they are seen by others, and think that this would come across as impressive. They might seek reinforcement from other people to prop up their self-image. Some who notice it might see an opportunity to exploit the observation and use ego-enhancement techniques and flattery to win their favor.

- **"To Make that Accomplishment, I had to Work Hard":** When someone takes the time to add a descriptive term such as "hard" in this case, it suggests that they place value upon accomplishments that are not very easy to achieve. This could indicate that the person speaking has just realized a goal that was harder to reach than other goals they have undertaken.

The fact that they use the word "hard" shows also that they know how to hold off on receiving gratification or believe in working hard and being dedicated to what they do. Someone who is applying for a job with this quality would probably be a great employee to hire due to their level of determination and the ability to tackle challenges.

- **"I was Patiently Waiting for this"**: The clue here is the word "patiently", which shows a few different things. Maybe the person speaking sat through something they were bored with, or had something important to attend to after their obligation. Whatever their reason for being patient, they were probably thinking of something other than what they were waiting through. Someone who has just waited patiently for something likely is aware of etiquette and the norms of politeness.

Someone who has something else to get to, but waits anyway, is adhering to social norms. A person who would not wait patiently likely does not adhere to these same norms, or is simply not as aware of them. When someone has this awareness, he or she will be great at their job and likely have respect for figures of authority. On the other hand, someone who is not aware of the norms of social behavior would be better suited for a job requiring creativity and thinking outside of boundaries.

- **"I Decided Upon this Option"**: Someone who talks about a decision they made indicates, by their word choice, that they had a few different choices before making their final decision. Maybe they struggled a bit first, which indicates that they prefer to consider their choices thoroughly before making any decision. This is especially telling if that person took time to think over their options when even it was a minor choice. Using "decided" in a sentence might also hint at the fact that they are not prone to impulsiveness.

Someone who is more impulsive in their choices would probably use words like "just" to describe what they did, indicating that they did it without much forethought. Someone using "decided" in their sentence may be more introverted, since introverts tend to think carefully over their choices rather than being on the impulsive side of the spectrum. This is not to say that a person who uses this word is definitely an introvert. However, it does give a hint to this possibility.

- **"I Made the Right Choice"**: The word choice "right" in a sentence like this indicates that the speaker underwent a struggle of an ethical, moral, or legal nature and experienced a bit of opposition (either external or internal), with the hopes of coming to the best choice. A personality trait such as this shows that the person is fairly strong inside and wants to make the right choice, even while undergoing some difficulty.

Of course, in order to know the full details of a person's personality, a complete assessment on a psychological scale would be needed. However, the word examples given above can give you a huge head start in analyzing different kinds people. In addition to this, any observer will be miles ahead in understanding someone if they figure out whether that person is an introvert or an extrovert.

Introversion vs. Extroversion:

Most people fall into either the introverted or extroverted category. Although some may fall closer to the middle of this spectrum, most are more one or the other. Let's look at some key differences in these personality types that will help you with your desire to analyze people accurately and effectively.

- **Extroversion:** People who are more extroverted tend to feel energized when around people and draw stimulation due to what their surroundings are like. This personality type tends to speak what comes to mind without overthinking their thoughts, and like to try things out first to figure out how they work. Rather than carefully considering each option thoroughly before acting, they tend to use quick judgment and deal with the consequences later.

  They are comfortable making decisions at the spur of the moment and are okay with acting impulsively sometimes. This personality type makes a great leader, due to their confident and self-assured nature. An extroverted person will likely prefer an exciting and fun environment with a lot of action and many people.

- **Introversion:** Introverts, on the other hand, use quite a bit of energy to be socially engaged, and they need time alone afterward in order to recharge and feel okay again. This personality type enjoys being alone, drawing inspiration and stimulation from alone time. They weigh their words carefully, along with their choices, before deciding on their final option. They must access information or knowledge and then digest it for a while before making a choice.

Pressuring an introvert for any reason is highly counterproductive and may simply lead them to shut down or say "no". Introverts are great idea people and often work in fields that rely on heavy creativity. When dealing with someone introverted, it's important to understand that they need time to think and will often prefer quiet environments over loud and boisterous ones.

It's rare that a person is completely introverted or completely extroverted, since this is a continuum and not meant to give you absolute information about someone. Most people show both introverted and extroverted traits in their personalities, or they may act more like an introvert in one situation and more like an extrovert in another. In addition, someone who is introverted, but not shy, may exhibit extroverted behaviors at times, while extroverts might act and feel more introverted in certain circumstances.

Using this Knowledge to Read People:

Once you are aware of the spectrum of introversion and extroversion, you are way ahead as far as understanding and analyzing people goes. This will help you predict the way someone may make decisions, the environments they prefer, and the way they like to spend their time. This, in combination with the words people use, can be used to effectively figure someone out, at least in a general sense.

CHAPTER 2: USING WORDS TO ANALYZE PEOPLE

Chapter 3: Interpreting Body Language Signals

Now that we have gone over what can be learned by someone's words, it's important to review and think about the communication that lies beneath: body language. People spend a lot of time figuring out how to read the nonverbal information that people send us. As we do this, they are likely doing the same to us, trying to figure out what our body language is saying beneath our words.

- **Showing Feelings:** At times, you may wish for your feelings to be overt and obvious, particularly in situations where these emotions are reciprocated and of a positive nature. However, this might be hard for some people, especially the types who don't feel comfortable expressing emotions and feelings. What people who are great at interpreting body language already know is that true feelings shine through, even if someone is not overtly trying to show them to the world.

- **Hiding Feelings:** There are times when we wish to hide our feelings from the world. This isn't always easy, especially when you are around people who are good at analyzing feelings and behavior. Learning how to keenly read body language will help you see emotional cues, even when someone is trying to hide them.

The Body's Role in Expressing Thoughts and Feelings:

Nonverbal communication (also known as body language), is exactly what it sounds like, your body's own language. Some may believe that feelings are only shown on the face, but this is only one tiny portion of the equation. Our whole bodies are constantly hiding or showing what we feel and a keen eye will pick up on this, even if we aren't aware of it ourselves. In order to hide it, you have to work very hard on taming the subconscious cues given by your body.

This chapter will tell you exactly how you can use someone's body parts to read what they are truly feeling on the inside. By the end of this chapter, you will have a better understanding of gestures, hidden messages, and signals of emotion hidden within the body. All of this is key to analyzing the feelings, thoughts, and behavior of the people around us.

Here are the most expressive parts of the human body (some may surprise you):

- **The Body Language Cues of the Head:** Beginning with the very top of the human body, the head is highly expressive and tells a lot about a person. Let's begin with the highest part of the body, which is the scalp, of course. A person's hair can tell a lot about their mental state at the time. When someone has messy hair, this can tell much about their mood. For example, when someone is stressed out, they might not take the time to tame their hair. This could show that they were in a hurry earlier that day, or are undergoing a tough emotional period in their life.

  Others can tell instantly when you are not feeling very "together" on any given day by this simple, yet very telling clue. When someone's hair is groomed, it gives a clue that they are at least somewhat in control. For people who don't have hair, their foreheads are more exposed than others, so moods can be read by this body part, along with the eyebrows. You can't really control what certain parts of your face look like, such as your nose, but there are some other parts of the face that give a lot away about a person's state of emotions.

- **Nonverbal Cues in the Micro-Expression Muscles:** The parts mentioned above are the muscles surrounding your mouth and eyes, which create tiny facial expressions. These are highly important in analyzing nonverbal expressions because they don't lie, even when someone is attempting to mask how they feel. Someone may wish to hide fearful feelings if they are speaking with a person to whom they wish to give a favorable impression, but a twitch of the muscles around the mouth will show that they are actually nervous.

    When someone just got a new haircut that you think is hideous, it will show in a twitch of your mouth, even if you try to smile and say that you like it. In order to get an idea of how comfortable or at ease someone feels in a certain situation, look at this area of the face. Is it calm and relaxed or tight?

- **What do the Eyes Tell us?:** This is quite an obvious one, but the eyes give a lot of important information about how someone feels inside. The most important factor in regard to the expressions of your eyes is the amount of eye contact given. There is a perfect balance between too little and too much eye contact, both of which tell you how someone is feeling. When someone is staring at you without taking a break from it, they seem overbearing and perhaps overly interested. A person who constantly looks away and seems reluctant to hold your gaze for more than a second, on the other hand, gives the impression of nervousness or disinterest.

Some people seem to have a constant twinkle in their eye, which communicates an open, friendly, and approachable personality that you feel comfortable talking with. Some people do this on purpose in order to create a favorable impression about themselves. They may do this to appear welcoming and approachable while having ulterior motives. When observing anyone's behavior, you must take into consideration the context, their typical disposition, and the immediate environment in order to get a complete understanding. We will go over this more in a later chapter.

- **The Body Language of the Neck and Chin:** Before covering the other body parts of nonverbal communication, we should cover a couple of parts that are not often thought of or observed when attempting to read or analyze others. Again, some facial features cannot be helped, and this should be considered when analyzing a person's face.

Someone who has a prominent jaw might look, at first glance, to be a bit stubborn and they may completely surprise you once you get to know them. It is more how they hold their chin that tells you what they're like. Do they seem to jut their chin out constantly, or do they keep it tucked in? This is an indication of confidence, or a lack of confidence.

The neck can also tell us quite a lot about a person's mental state. If they are using it to hold their head upright, staring straight ahead, it indicates confidence and a poised state of mind. If the neck is drooping, however, this shows a low mood or a lack of confidence. A person who has a habit of doing this likely suffers from a low self-image or problems with being shy. A person who does not usually do this, but is seen doing it, is likely encountering some type of stress at the moment.

- **What the Core of the Body or Torso Says about Emotions:** If someone is using their neck to hold their head up high, they might also be walking with an erect posture. When someone has their shoulders back and their back quite straight, this indicates that they are in control of their emotions, or at least they wish to appear this way. On the flip side, someone who is not sitting up straight and appears to be sagging might be in a deflated mood or wishing to appeal to the sympathy of other people. Again, this is situational, and how often someone appears this way says a lot.

If someone is constantly sagging and does not walk upright, it indicates that they don't feel great about themselves. In addition, slouching will lead to issues with health. Parents constantly telling their kids to sit up straight and stop slouching are actually correct. Standing upright, yet portraying an easy and relaxed demeanor, shows confidence and a self-assured state of mind, so keep an eye on posture if you want to understand how someone feels about themselves.

- **The Nonverbal Cues of the Upper Limbs:** The next part of the body that displays a person's state of mind is the hands and arms. Although you may not consciously pay much attention to these parts, they show a lot about how a person is feeling at the time. When someone has their arms crossed, they are displaying frustration or an aggressive state of mind. When someone is fidgeting with their bands, they are showing boredom or anxiety. Someone standing with their hands on their hips gives the impression of over-confidence or arrogance.

When people are feeling relaxed, confident, and positive, their arms and hands tend to communicate this by looking neutral. A neutral position of the hands or arms is one that is not tense or rigid, but not restless and fidgety either. You can tell that someone is feeling comfortable when they are sitting down with their hands held in their lap, not clutching them together, but just gently clasping them.

- **More about the Arms:** These body parts are perhaps the most telling of all when it comes to analyzing a person's true feelings or thoughts in any given situation. Some gestures of the arms are ingrained in us at a young age (like the fact that it's rude to point at strangers). However, the key factors to be aware of here are how high a person's arms reach into the air and the amount of space the person's arms are occupying. Gestures of the body that defy gravity are typically very positive and this is especially true when it comes to the arms.

When someone is interested, excited, or happy, they lift up their chins or head, their arms begin moving upward, and even their feet and legs will start to point up or bounce if they are sitting down. A person's arms are highly versatile at showing emotion. Watch a person when they are happy or excited, and their arms move in an unrestricted fashion moving their arms above their faces, seemingly in spite of gravity.

This is quite an intuitive association. When someone is feeling positive, their body makes upward gestures that seem to defy gravity. If someone is in a confident mood and feeling good about themselves, their arms will naturally swing easily as they walk. Someone who is low in confidence or feeling uncomfortable will typically restrain their arms subconsciously. Watch someone as they receive negative news about a mistake they made and their arms and shoulders will immediately move toward the floor.

We often hear and talk about a "sinking" emotion in regards to negative events and this is a hardwired, innate limbic reaction. Bad feelings will bring you down not just mentally, but physically, and can be seen to observers who know what to look for. These responses are honest and immediate. Someone will thrust their fists and arms up into the air when something good happens, but allow their arms and shoulders to droop when something negative occurs.

Pay attention to gravity when watching a person's body

language and you will be able to read how they are feeling quite accurately. These movements occur immediately as the emotion arises. In addition to this, these motions are contagious, especially in a group of people who know each other or have all gathered for a particular event (such as a concert or sports event).

- **The Body Language of the Legs:** Now that we've covered the upper limbs, we can move onto the lower part of the bod--the legs. Any time a person you are observing is able to be seen fully, either standing or sitting, they are giving obvious displays of what they are feeling inside. Crossing your legs tightly as you sit down shows that you are closing yourself off to the world, subconsciously attempting to protect yourself mentally. When someone has their legs splayed out in a careless and relaxed fashion, it shows the opposite.

A person can show that they are feeling confident and relaxed with an easy posture of the legs, but too much might show that they are bored or even sloppy. A nervous state of mind comes across quite clearly when someone is tapping their feet nervously, showing that they are irritated or perhaps just anxious. This is the biggest area of someone's body, so it's quite telling how much they move or do not move the legs. Someone who has their legs gently crossed, rather than tightly, is giving the impression of relaxed and poised self-confidence.

- **What do the Feet say about your Mental State?** Since the feet are the lowest part of the body, it's a good place to end the list of body parts of nonverbal communication. As mentioned earlier, restless legs show that someone is nervous or anxious, which includes restless feet as well. However, a lot can be shown by simply observing what someone's feet are doing separately. Someone who taps their foot restlessly is likely in a hurry or wishes to leave the place they are to get somewhere else. They might also do this as a way to grab the attention of someone else.

    This is a small, subtle way to show that someone is in a rush without being rude about it. In addition, a person's feet can also project the level of fear or confidence they are feeling. When someone walks strong and steady, they are likely self-assured or feeling good about themselves. As mentioned earlier, slouching shows the exact opposite. You can also tell a lot about a person's true mood and feelings by looking at where their feet are pointing. The feet show our subconscious "fight or flight" tendencies.

This means that when someone is in a situation they wish to escape (even subconsciously), their feet will be pointing away from the person they are talking to.

Someone who is engaged in a conversation with their feet pointing toward the person they are speaking with on the other hand clearly wants to be where they are. If you wish to know where you stand with someone, simply check out which direction their feet are pointing next time the two of you are conversing. In addition, you can tell the level of rapport two people are sharing by seeing at which direction their feet are pointing. If they are pointing toward each other, they are both satisfied with the conversation and being around each other.

A Summary of Body Language Cues:

The body parts covered in this chapter are meant to give you some food for thought as far as analyzing people and observing their emotions goes. In addition to using this information to better understand those around you, you can also use it to affect the image you are portraying to the world. Try observing people that you don't know while out in public first and then move onto your friends. The plus side of observing the emotions of your friends is the fact that you can confirm your suspicions afterward by asking them if you were right.

The actions of a person's body show, unconsciously and consciously, what they are feeling inside. Learning how to observe these subtle cues will give you a peek inside the brain of anyone you choose to analyze. But there are some considerations to keep in mind if you want to be more accurate with your suspicions, judgments, and observations of nonverbal cues:

- **The Environment:** Although body language can tell a lot about how someone is feeling, or the type of person they are, the environment they are in at the time should also be considered. Perhaps someone appears to be anxious or fearful for some reason. This may lead you to make the mistaken assumption that they are, by nature, a nervous person, but this is not necessarily the case. Perhaps they are under stress for a specific reason and typically they are very calm.

    Taking this into consideration, you can only understand a person's disposition by considering which factors in their life at that moment are influencing how they act and the way they feel. For example, you might see someone who appears very deflated, walking in a slouching manner, and draw the conclusion that they have a low level of self-confidence. Keep in mind that this is not necessarily true and that perhaps they have just received devastating news or missed a job offer they were hoping for.

They key to accurately reading someone is taking into consideration not only body language cues or nonverbal signals, but also the situation they are currently dealing with. This takes a bit more observation and thinking than a split-second judgment, but that's what it takes to efficiently analyze people.

- **Personality:** In addition to a person's body language cues, and the environment they are current in, their personality also plays an important role in the way they behave on a day to day basis. Seeing someone in one situation, it can be easy to make an assumption about what they are like; but once you get to know someone more, you might learn that their personality was the key influence on how they were acting. The best way to accurately judge or analyze a person's behavior is to understand their innate personality traits.

This takes time since getting to know someone doesn't happen instantly. This means that in order to truly read someone, you have to understand their true characteristics. Although you can gain some insight into a person's nature by observing them as a stranger, it's only through knowing them on a personal level that you can truly gauge who they are, how they feel, and why they feel that way.

Body Language Myth vs. Truth:

Due to certain shows on television, among other factors, people have a lot of misconceptions about how nonverbal communication works. In order to accurately understand this language, this should be cleared up. Here are some truths you probably didn't know about the subject:

- **Gestures can be Ambiguous:** One huge misunderstanding about nonverbal communication is that gestures always mean something specific, but the fact is that gestures are usually quite ambiguous. They have multiple meanings, depending on the context. This is important to remember since you could assume someone is being defensive by crossing their arms, for example, when they are actually just cold. Where is this huge misunderstanding really coming from? Experts on television who wish to sound as though they have it all figured out often give analyses in the heat of the moment. This can be anything from an analysis of a celebrity's behavior in an interview to a presidential candidate's facial expressions during a speech.

The second culprit of this widespread myth is the history of nonverbal communication and the way it has been studied. This started with specific gestures which carry certain meanings behind them, such as a "thumbs up" or "okay" sign. This has resulted in a bias toward all gestures having specified meanings that apply to everyone. However, gestures vary across different cultures and don't necessarily have specified meanings at all outside their original country.

- **The Rest of the Body is more Truthful than the Face:** A person who is not familiar with the subject of body language might assume that the face is the most logical place to begin when you are trying to read someone's feelings or thoughts. However, kids learn at a young age to hide what they really feel, often for the sake of politeness or social norms. This could result in smiling by default, even if we aren't happy, pretending to care about the small talk in your office, and more.

This doesn't mean that people are perfect at hiding their true feelings; but most of the time, our face is not an accurate portrayal of our feelings. This, however, has its purpose, helping us avoid conflict and get through social interactions and work smoothly on a day to day basis. When you are trying to read a person's true feelings, make sure you pay attention to what their entire body is saying, using the clues we gave you above about the legs, the arms, and so on.

- **It's about Intention, not Specifics:** Typically, nonverbal cues in other people can show us what they are intending, and not always what the reason for this intention is. What this unspoken language can tell us in a quite efficient and accurate way is the intention of feeling a person has. Actually, studies have shown that the emotions we feel appear in our physical bodies first and in the conscious brain second. This means that when you are excited, impatient, tired, or hungry, your body already knows this and starts portraying it immediately.

This means that learning the art of nonverbal communication and reading body language relies on seeking what the intentions of others are. Once you establish this, you can figure out more specific thoughts they have behind these intentions, as well as the emotions and ideas that logically follow or result. Although the majority of people are decently skilled at hiding their feelings on their faces, they are not as talented with hiding it in their bodies, since the body already knows before they do.

As your conscious brain is finally recognizing joy or anger, it has already appeared physically, and these are the clues you should be searching for when you analyze and read the people around you. If you allow this to sink in, you will be miles ahead of other people in reading body language, which brings me to my next point.

- **This is a Largely Intuitive Skill:** You might be a lot more talented at this than you believe. When it comes to people you're already familiar with and know on a day to day basis, you are better than an expert at interpreting their intentions. Consider this, you are already aware of it when your partner is mad at you, when your kid is feeling fussy or bored, or when your manager is feeling stressed out about a deadline. When it comes to people you already know, you've gathered hours' worth of study material about them and already recognize their clues and signals. There is, of course, the possibility that these people could lie to us, but when it comes to important issues, it is not for very long.

- **Think Less about it:** This might sound counterintuitive, after all; why would you want to think less about something you're trying to improve upon and master? But in order to get better at reading nonverbal signals and cues, try not to think about it too much. Humans are already designed to read the intentions and emotions of other people. Our brains all come equipped with mirror neurons that allow us to feel what another person is feeling and instantly recognize it for what it is.

  This feeling gets mirrored in our brains, allowing us to understand where they are coming from. This has developed throughout evolution and has contributed widely to our survival in our early days. As soon as a person sees another person feeling fear, they instantly react and subconsciously get ready to rise to action when needed. We are already experts at reading other people, but this knowledge must be brought to your conscious brain from the subconscious level.

In order to make use of this expertise, just inquire within your subconscious brain and allow the answer to come to you. Since you are already aware of what it is, you just have to let yourself realize it. Your brain is always reading the emotional content of the people you're around throughout the day, and it's only a matter of believing in your instincts. This might take practice, but it gets easier with time and once you become aware, you will improve quite fast.

Chapter 3: Interpreting Body Language Signals

Chapter 4: Using a Comfort vs. Discomfort Spectrum

As mentioned in the previous chapter, the body language a person displays shows a lot about their inner world and feelings at the moment. It also plays a huge role in our communication with the people around us. But the majority of people have only a basic, intuitive understanding of body language. Luckily, if interpreting these nonverbal clues is not easy or simple for you, or if you wish to improve in this area, a lot of information exists out there that can help you understand this.

Paying attention to what a person's body is saying is a key factor in analyzing their behavior and interpreting their feelings and thoughts, but it's not that simple. We already reviewed a bit about which body parts can give us clues to a person's thoughts and feelings, but there is something else to be taken into account here. Remembering these key points will help you take your analysis and understanding to a whole new level.

The Comfort vs. Discomfort Spectrum for Understanding Body Language:

Many people believe that once they finally understand the world of nonverbal communication and cues, they will be able to tell who is lying at all times. Although this is an understandable desire, it's not possible to accurately read someone based on body language alone. The best way to interpret how they really feel is to pay attention to their comfort or discomfort levels. The spectrum of comfort vs. discomfort gives us far more leverage in understanding what a person's expressions really mean.

- **Why Comfort Matters in Reading Others:** When someone is guilty about something, or being deceitful in some way, they have to live with that knowledge; and most people will find it hard to feel comfortable with this. It means that their crimes or deception will make it difficult to feel at ease with themselves or the situation, making their distress easy to spot. The attempt to hide this deception or guilt will place a huge stress on their minds as they attempt to come up with answers that should sound natural; it should be simple, but they are not due to the perceived necessity to lie.

If someone feels comfortable talking with you, it will be quite simple to find out when they are being dishonest. The goal here should be to get to a level of ease and rapport that allows them to feel comfortable talking with you. Once you establish this baseline, by showing you how they act naturally, when no threats are present, you can accurately read them.

- **Context is Key in Analyzing People**: Although this is a useful tool for figuring out when someone is deceiving you or lying, this trick sets the stage for interpreting all nonverbal cues and body language. Take for instance a situation when you are at a social event surrounded by people having a good time. Noticing someone in the corner, sitting down with folded arms, will stand out to you. That person may appear to be ill at ease, leading you to wonder if something is wrong or off with them.

Noticing this would likely lead you to inquire whether something is going wrong with that person. However, take this same scenario as observed in the waiting room of a hospital. It would not stand out whatsoever, and you might even expect to see this in such a place. You likely wouldn't ask someone if something is wrong if you were in a hospital, because it would seem obvious why they display a particular body language.

- **When you Already Know Someone:** Some people wish to learn how to analyze others because they wish to understand strangers on a deeper level. Others want to understand the people they already know in a more intimate way. If the latter applies to you, you already know how the person acts when they are comfortable. This means that you should be able to accurately read them and that they key in doing this lies in looking past your bias.

For example, perhaps you have known someone for years and you wish to know whether they are happy in a given situation. Your bias of thinking of this person as close to you and always in your good favor may make it harder to see what they are truly feeling, whether it is annoyance or wishing for more space. On the other hand, you might have a relative who you believe does not like you, and may be blind to true understanding when they are actually being kind to you.

Taking into account the personal relationship you have with the person is very important when it comes to interpreting their emotions or thoughts. If you have known someone for a very long time, you see them in a certain light; and this will always affect how you read their disposition and body language.

Paying attention to a person's comfort level in specific situations tells us a lot about their feelings. When going out on a date with someone you like for the first time, and seeing that they appear to feel at ease with you, can give you a hint that they probably like you. If you're giving someone an interview for a job, and the applicant appears confident and comfortable but suddenly appears anxious when you ask about whether they have committed theft in the past, this could give you a clue to something important. Although nonverbal cues and body language reading is not a hard science, all of this information in combination can give you valuable hints about what someone is thinking.

Situations for Gauging Comfort Levels:

There are a few different situations that can be revealing about the way someone acts when they are comfortable, which will help you recognize when they are feeling strong emotions other than comfort. Here are some examples to start with:

- **Get them Talking about Something Pleasant:** When someone is in a good mood, having a relaxing conversation about a pleasant topic, this is a great time to check on how they act while at ease. You could start by asking them what their passion is, what their interests are, or something neutral such as what they do for work.

- **Ask Open-Ended Questions:** It's hard to get a conversation flowing or gauge how someone acts when they are comfortable if you only ask them "yes or no" questions. Make sure you ask them questions that require at least a sentence or two to answer, so you have time to listen to their speech patterns, notice their mannerisms, and in general see how they act while at ease.

- **Go on a Walk:** Having a conversation with someone as you are sitting down across from one another can be a bit intimidating to some, especially if it is someone you don't know very well. A better way to get to know a person's mannerisms is to talk to them while on a walk. This allows the thoughts and words to flow more freely, giving you a more accurate picture of who they really are.

Once you find out who someone is when they are in a neutral or basically positive mood, you will notice when a strong feeling appears since you have already established a baseline. Analyzing someone basically means knowing how to identify when they are feeling or thinking something specific, so this is absolutely essential to learning this skill. Establish the baseline first, then notice when it changes. This is key in analyzing people in an accurate way.

Chapter 5: Understanding yourself First

In order to accurately read other people, we must first know how to read our own emotions and thoughts. After all, what is the goal behind analyzing others? It's to develop a deeper understanding of humanity, and this desire is incomplete if it doesn't include ourselves. Understanding your own emotions is important for countless reasons: career success, healthy relationships, and living a peaceful existence in general. But it will also help you in understanding all social dynamics you are surrounded by. Let's look first at the consequences of not understanding yourself.

What do Unrecognized Emotions Result in?

When we bury or repress our feelings, by not taking the time to understand them or ourselves, serious issues exist not only mentally, but physically as a result. Not taking the time to pay attention to and deal with your emotions will affect your mentality, ability to develop and grow as a person, and your personal relationships.

- **Physical Consequences:** Repressing or ignoring your emotions on a long-term basis will lead to serious issues, such as permanent fatigue, arthritis, or lowered immunity. Studies show that your mentality directly relates to your ability to heal from serious illnesses. People with serious physical health issues have trouble with everything in life, including accurate judgment when it comes to interpreting the behavior, thoughts, and moods of others. If you wish to get better in this area, you must first notice your own emotions.

- **A Lowered Ability to Accurately Read Others:** When you don't pay attention to your own feelings, you cannot accurately judge what you observe in other people. If your goal is to analyze other people and understand what they think and feel, you must first have a logical perspective about yourself. For example, if you struggle with insecurity and don't believe in yourself, you will likely interpret someone else's actions as negative towards you when they don't necessarily show this.

To have sharp perceptive skills of observation, you need

mental energy and keeping emotions buried burns off this mental energy. This means that you don't have the stamina necessary to perform other mental tasks, even something as simple as accurately gauging what others are thinking or feeling.

How to Learn More about yourself:

A person who decides to get healthy on an emotional level and understand themselves truly is committed to this path and willing to do whatever it takes. Although this is not always comfortable or easy, you will become much smarter and observant about others once you undertake it. Feelings are the most reliable way to figure out what is happening inside of your mind. Many methods exist for identifying your emotions, meaning that you can pick the method that works best for you.

While some people find that it's easiest to do this alone, others find it helpful to combine it with observing other people. Some people may find journaling helpful, while others prefer not to write about emotions. For most people, a combination of multiple methods works best. What follows are some general guidelines for figuring out your own thoughts about feelings regarding a particular situation or person.

Becoming Aware:

In order to understand and analyze others, you first have to become aware of yourself. This is the first step to making progress in any pursuit in life. Here are some steps to doing this:

- **Paying Attention to Thoughts:** The best way to start getting to know yourself better is to start paying attention to your own thoughts throughout the day. Most people get so used to thinking a certain way that they don't notice what is going on in their own heads. Pay attention to every little detail and stay aware of what your thoughts are. This is a great way to learn more about the way your mind works, how you truly feel about your relationships, and what you like and dislike. Although many believe that they already know these things about themselves, looking a bit deeper may surprise you, and there is always more to learn.

- **Journaling:** One great way to stay aware of your thoughts is to start keeping a journal and write every day, even if it's only a small amount. You can then look back on these entries and learn a great deal about yourself and the way your thoughts and feelings function. This will help you recognize the thoughts and feelings of others and become better at analyzing their behavior. The better you get at reading your own thoughts and feelings, the better you will be at reading the thoughts and feelings of the people in your life who you wish to analyze.

- **Figure out what "doesn't Matter" to you:** Most people have a list of things in their life that they claim don't matter or are not a big deal when, in fact, something is bothering them quite a lot. This leads to repression and denial of your own feelings and thoughts and makes it hard to digest the information. This leads to confusion and turmoil inside and makes it hard to tell right from left. Start by making a list of those small things that "don't matter" but actually keep popping up for you.

Anything that seems to appear repeatedly but cannot be easily explained away should go on your list. A lot of people have a long list of items from the time they were small children, which leads to mental issues and health problems later in life. Taking the time to identify these "small and meaningless" matters that will help you learn about your own emotions and the best way to deal with them.

- **Notice what Elicits Strong Feelings in you:** Start paying attention to different matters in your life that elicit strong feelings in you for a few weeks. This can be a person, certain weather, or politics; anything that makes you have strong emotions, good or bad, must be recorded. This is a great way to become emotionally healthy and understand yourself as well as others in a deeper way. Once you recognize what makes you feel strong and know how to identify when this happens, you will be able to recognize the same feelings in those around you.

  Recognizing emotions is part of what analyzing people is all about, since you have to know how to identify an emotion in order to notice that it's there in the first place. Once you can label and deal with your own feelings, you will be better equipped to label and deal with the feelings of others. This includes both positive and negative emotions and everything that lies in between.

- **Pay Attention to Memories:** Everyone has recurring memories that never seem to go away, no matter how much time has passed. This could be related to a situation or a person from your past. Although it isn't quite comfortable to do this, you should intentionally remember these incidents and allow yourself to feel the pain surrounding them. Write extensively about what this is like since these memories are likely contributing to a mental distress that you are not even aware of.

- **Get Specific about your Feelings:** As mentioned a bit earlier, part of noticing the emotions of others is knowing how to identify them specifically. Before you can be any good at identifying other people's emotions, you first need to learn how to identify your own. This begins with getting specific. Ask yourself not only what you are feeling, but why, and any details about it. Many people get confused trying to become familiar with their feelings since they are too general in describing them.

Staying general about feelings doesn't really help at all because it doesn't offer any solution. Once you figure out specifically what you feel and why you feel it, you can effectively deal with your emotions. This will help you recognize the feelings of others and also help them deal with them, which is part of the appeal of learning how to analyze people.

- **Know your Positive Feelings:** It's important that you know how to pay attention to your positive feelings as well as your negative ones. Most people are generous, forgiving, and compassionate multiple times throughout their days. Make sure that as you get to know your own mind, you are giving yourself credit for these emotions, which will allow you to see a fuller picture of who you are as a person. Once you can identify these feelings in yourself, they are easier to see and recognize in the people around you. Remember to keep a balance by accurately looking at the entire spectrum rather than being biased toward either positive or negative thoughts and feelings.

- **Hone your Intuition**: As we mentioned in the chapter about body language, you are already an expert at analyzing the thoughts and feelings of other people due to the way we have all evolved as humans. It is simply a matter of getting in touch with this innate wisdom. Set aside some time each day to get in touch with your own instincts, learning how to listen to them and believing what they are telling you. This will make you a lot more perceptive and observant when it comes to reading yourself and others.

The best time to start doing this practice is during the morning when you have some quiet time to think undisturbed. This allows you to get in touch with your mind before the chaos of the day begins or your schedule and work duties catch up with you. If you take the time to get in touch with silence and your own mind, this peace will follow you throughout the rest of the day and your judgments and observations will be much more accurate, thorough, and keen.

- **Talk with Friends**: Friends are a valuable resource when it comes to both understanding ourselves and others better. If you have a friend who is also interested in learning how to accurately analyze people, that's even better. You can compare your findings, observations, and notes with each other and practice together. Throughout the day, stop a few times to try to read what your friend is thinking or feeling and confirm whether you were correct. Have them do the same to you; it will provide great practice for both of you in learning how to better analyze people.

CHAPTER 5: UNDERSTANDING YOURSELF FIRST

Conclusion

Thank you again for buying this book!

I hope this book was able to help you to see the endless possibilities that become available to you once you know how to read and analyze those around you. Many people struggle through life because they have not realized the simple steps to harnessing this power. You are now a few steps ahead and can begin transforming your life with this knowledge. Once you know how to analyze the people in your life, including mere acquaintances and even strangers, the world is yours. Remember that the key lies in practicing. This book has given you the tools to get a great start and now it's up to you to put in the effort and utilize this great information.

The next step is to start using some of this new information to better yourself, those around you and to accomplish your goals. With this information, you are only limited by what your own imagination can come up with.

Thank you!

Thank you for buying *How To Analyze People*. If you enjoyed reading this book, then I'd like to ask you for a favor, **would you be kind enough to leave a review for this book on Amazon? It'd be greatly appreciated!**

All my best wishes,

Kevin Bradnik

www.ingramcontent.com/pod-product-compliance
Lightning Source LLC
Chambersburg PA
CBHW061203180526
45170CB00002B/940